Elliot GETS STUCK

For Jack

Elliot Moose

Elliot Moose™ Andrea Beck Inc.
Text and illustrations © 2002 Andrea Beck Inc.

Kids Can Press acknowledges the financial support of the Ontario Arts Council, the Canada Council for the Arts and the Government of Canada, through the BPIDP, for our publishing activity.

Published in Canada by
Kids Can Press Ltd.
29 Birch Avenue
Toronto, ON M4V 1E2

Published in the U.S. by
Kids Can Press Ltd.
2250 Military Road
Tonawanda, NY 14150

www.kidscanpress.com

The artwork in this book was rendered in pencil crayon. The text is set in Minion.

Edited by Debbie Rogosin
Designed by Karen Powers
Printed and bound in Hong Kong by Book Art Inc., Toronto
This book is smyth sewn casebound.

CM 02 0 9 8 7 6 5 4 3 2 1

National Library of Canada Cataloguing in Publication Data

Beck, Andrea, 1956–
    Elliot gets stuck

"An Elliot Moose story."

ISBN 1-55337-014-7

I. Title.

PS8553.E2948E432 2002   jC813'.54   C2001-901002-8
PZ7.B380767Elg 2002

Kids Can Press is a Nelvana company

Elliot
GETS STUCK

Written and Illustrated by

ANDREA BECK

KIDS CAN PRESS

Elliot Moose

woke up with his nose twitching and his feet itching.
He ran to the big front door, looked through the letter
slot and grinned from ear to ear.

"It's spring!" he whooped.

The snow was melting. There were rivers and
puddles everywhere. He and Socks could build dams
and race twig boats today!

"Socks," called Elliot.
"Spring is here. Let's go
outside!"

He hurried to the kitchen and pushed on
the doggy door, but it was still jammed with
ice. They'd have to use the big front door.

"Come on, Socks!" Elliot shouted
as he ran back. "I need help with
the door."

Skidding to a stop, Elliot looked up at the door handle. He wished he could climb like Socks — then he wouldn't have to wait for her to turn the knob.

Elliot took another peek through the letter slot. Then he poked his nose into the opening and twisted and turned until he managed to squeeze his whole head through.

What a glorious day!

Elliot wormed his arms through the slot and began to pull himself forward. Wouldn't Socks be surprised if he got outside by himself!

Elliot took a deep breath and pulled harder. He managed to wriggle his shoulders through. But his tummy just wouldn't fit.

He'd have to wait for help after all.

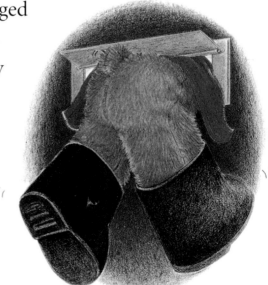

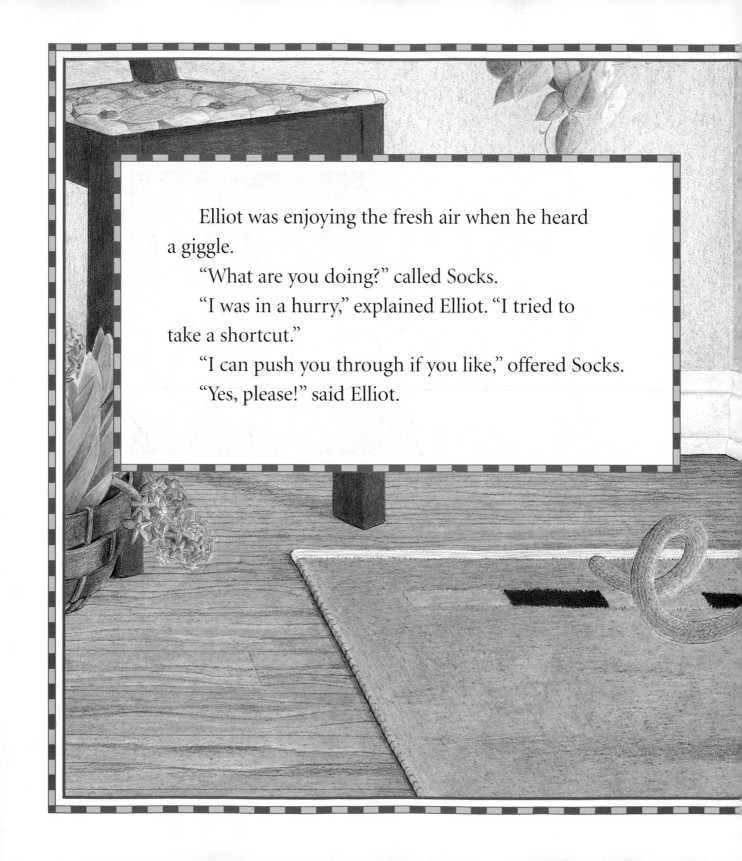

Elliot was enjoying the fresh air when he heard a giggle.

"What are you doing?" called Socks.

"I was in a hurry," explained Elliot. "I tried to take a shortcut."

"I can push you through if you like," offered Socks.

"Yes, please!" said Elliot.

But when Socks pushed,
Elliot barely moved.
"Try again," he said.
Socks used her shoulder
this time and pushed very hard.
But that only wedged Elliot tighter.

"I'm going to pull you back in," said Socks.
She grabbed Elliot's feet and tugged.
His tummy came free, but the
rest of him did not.
"Can you pull any
harder?" he asked.
Socks pulled with
all her might. But
Elliot did not budge.
He was stuck.

"I'll get help!" said Socks, and she hurried off
to find Amy.

Amy held on to Socks and Socks held on to Elliot.

They pulled and pulled with all their might.

But Elliot didn't move.

"Can you pull any harder?" he asked.

Amy went to get Paisley.

Paisley held on to Amy.

Amy held on to Socks.

And Socks held on to Elliot.

They pulled and pulled with all their might.

But Elliot still didn't move.

"You need to pull harder," he said.

Paisley went to get Angel.

Angel held on to Paisley.

Paisley held on to Amy.

Amy held on to Socks.

And Socks held on to Elliot.

They pulled and pulled with all their might.

But Elliot *still* did not come free.

Now he was worried.

"Please pull harder!" he begged.

"Hang on, Elliot," said Angel, and she went
to get the cubs.

The cubs held on to Angel, who held on to Paisley, who held on to Amy, who held on to Socks. Socks held on to Elliot.

They pulled and pulled with all their might.

But it was no use.

"I'm going to be stuck here forever!" Elliot cried.

Socks gave him a gentle pat. "Don't worry, Elliot," she said. "We'll think of something."

The friends began to talk.
Elliot overheard the words
"scissors," "saw" and "grease."
What were they planning?!
He stewed for a moment.
How had he fit into the slot?
Suddenly Elliot grinned.
"I wriggled!" he said,
wriggling. "And I wormed."
Slowly but surely, Elliot wormed his arms back
through the slot.
"I twisted!" he said, twisting. "And I turned."
Elliot turned his long nose sideways and pulled.
But he did not come free.

Elliot braced his paws against the door and took a deep breath.

"I wriggled and I wormed. I twisted … and … I … turned," he said, pushing with all his might.

POP!

Elliot flew backward through the air and landed next to his friends.

KERPLOP!

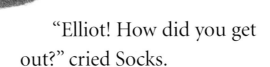

"Elliot! How did you get
out?" cried Socks.

"The same way I got in,"
laughed Elliot.

Everyone cheered.

Then Elliot jumped up. "It's spring!" he shouted.
"The sun is shining. The snow is melting. The birds
are singing. Let's go outside!"

They all ran to find coats and boots.

Then Socks turned the handle of the big front door.

And Elliot, Socks, Amy, Paisley, Angel and the cubs
all went out to play.

They splashed in puddles, built pebble dams and
raced twig boats.
It was a wonderful, warm first day of spring.